On Track Early

Family Alignment and Support Guide

A Practical System for Supporting Youth, Reinforcing Expectations, and Building Consistency at Home

North Star Practical Guides

Copyright © 2026 | All Rights Reserved

IMPORTANT NOTICE

This guide is for educational purposes only. It does not constitute legal advice, parenting instruction, mental health counseling, or clinical treatment. It does not replace requirements set by courts, probation officers, program staff, school officials, or any authority with jurisdiction over the youth referenced in this guide. All program requirements and conditions must be confirmed directly with the appropriate supervising authority.

THEORETICAL FOUNDATION: RISK-NEED-RESPONSIVITY FRAMEWORK

This guide is built on the Risk-Need-Responsivity (RNR) framework, the most extensively validated model in juvenile and criminal justice intervention research. Developed by Andrews, Bonta, and Hoge, the RNR framework identifies the principles that most reliably produce behavior change in structured populations. Every section of this guide is designed in alignment with those principles.

RISK PRINCIPLE

Match the intensity of intervention to the level of risk.

Higher-risk youth require more structured, intensive tools. This guide is designed for use in structured environments precisely because the youth who need it most benefit from consistent, daily-use systems rather than occasional instruction. Family dysfunction and inconsistent home structure are among the strongest predictors of continued system involvement for juvenile populations. This guide addresses that risk factor directly by giving families a practical alignment system.

NEED PRINCIPLE

Target the criminogenic needs that drive behavior.

Criminogenic needs are the dynamic factors most directly linked to continued system involvement. These include antisocial attitudes, poor self-regulation, weak problem-solving skills, antisocial peer associations, and family dysfunction. Family factors are a primary criminogenic need domain in the RNR model. When home expectations conflict with program expectations, youth receive contradictory signals that undermine the intervention. This guide closes that gap by aligning the family system with the program environment.

RESPONSIVITY PRINCIPLE

Deliver intervention in a way youth can actually learn from.

General responsivity requires using cognitive-behavioral, skills-based approaches rather than passive instruction. Specific responsivity requires matching delivery to the individual. The FIRM Framework applies the same cognitive-behavioral pause-and-respond structure to guardians that program staff use with youth. Consistent modeling of structured decision-making at home reinforces what youth are learning in their program.

SUPPORTING FRAMEWORKS

In addition to the RNR framework, this guide incorporates Core Correctional Practices (CCP), which emphasize relationship-based skill building; Cognitive-Behavioral Intervention principles, which connect thinking patterns to behavior and outcomes; and Desistance-Focused Supervision principles, which build identity and agency alongside compliance. Together these frameworks represent the current gold standard in evidence-based intervention for structured youth populations.

SECTION 1: INTRODUCTION AND PURPOSE

What This Guide Is

This guide is built for parents, guardians, and the adults who support youth in structured programs. It gives you a practical system for reinforcing the same expectations your youth faces in their program, at home, consistently, every day.

Why Family Alignment Changes Outcomes

Youth do not fail programs in isolation. When home expectations conflict with program expectations, youth receive mixed signals about what the standard actually is. When family members undermine accountability, even unintentionally, they create the conditions for failure. When the home environment and the program environment operate from the same framework, youth have a genuine foundation for success.

What This Guide Is Not

- Not parenting advice or personal criticism
- Not therapy or counseling for the family
- Not a replacement for program requirements or legal obligations
- Not a guarantee of any outcome

How to Use This Guide

Work through each section. Use the worksheets to assess your current approach. Use the trackers to build daily and weekly consistency. Use the check-in sections to create a structured communication habit with your youth. The more consistently you apply this system, the more effective your support will be.

KEY PRINCIPLE:

Consistency between home and program expectations leads to better outcomes for youth. This guide helps you build that consistency deliberately.

SECTION 2: UNDERSTANDING YOUR ROLE AS A SUPPORT SYSTEM

Your role as a parent or guardian in the context of a structured program is specific. It is not to be your youth's friend, their lawyer, or their shield from consequences. It is to be a stable, consistent source of structure, accountability, and genuine support, which is different from protection from outcomes.

What Effective Support Looks Like

- Holding your youth to the same expectations their program holds them to
- Following through consistently, not just when you have energy or patience
- Communicating clearly and calmly, even when the situation is emotional
- Staying connected to what is actually required of your youth, not just what they tell you
- Supporting the youth, not defending their behavior when accountability is appropriate

Common Patterns That Undermine Youth Progress

- Giving mixed messages, different standards on different days depending on your mood
- Making exceptions to requirements because it is inconvenient or because the youth pushes back
- Siding with the youth against the program without full information

- Letting guilt, love, or emotional pressure override accountability
- Assuming the program is handling everything and your role at home does not matter

Guardian Self-Assessment

Answer these questions honestly. They are for your own awareness, not for anyone else to evaluate.

Do I follow through consistently when I set an expectation?

Do I know the specific requirements my youth is under right now?

Do I communicate calmly when I am frustrated with my youth?

Have I ever removed a consequence because my youth pushed back hard enough?

Do the expectations I set at home match what their program requires?

What is one pattern I know I need to change to be more effective?

KEY PRINCIPLE:

Your consistency is your youth's foundation. Support works best when it is structured, predictable, and followed through every time.

SECTION 3: ALIGNING HOME EXPECTATIONS WITH PROGRAM EXPECTATIONS

Misalignment between home and program expectations is one of the most common and most preventable causes of youth failure in structured programs. When a youth hears one standard from their officer or program staff and a different standard at home, they default to whichever is less demanding, and that is rarely the one that keeps them on track.

What You Need to Know First

- The specific conditions your youth is required to follow, in writing, not just from memory
- Who their primary contact is at the program and how to reach them
- What is expected around curfew, attendance, associations, substance use, and reporting
- What the consequences are for specific violations, so you can reinforce, not contradict, them
- How often you are expected to communicate with the program as a family member

Program Contact Information

Program name:

____

Primary contact name and title:

____

Contact phone:

____

Contact email:

____

Check-in frequency (how often you should communicate with the program):

____

Reporting requirements (what you are responsible for reporting and when):

____

Expectation Alignment Worksheet

For each area, record what the program requires and confirm your home standard matches it.

Expectation Area	Program Requirement	Home Standard	Aligned? (Y/N)
Curfew			
School or program attendance			
Approved associations (who they can spend time with)			
Substance-free requirement			

Reporting requirements			
Technology and social media use			
Employment or community service obligations			
Other program-specific conditions			

KEY PRINCIPLE:
Youth respond better when expectations are clear and consistent across every environment they operate in. If home says one thing and the program says another, the youth will find the gap and use it.

SECTION 4: DECISION PATH: HOW TO RESPOND

How you respond to situations involving your youth sets the standard for how they learn to respond to situations in their own life. Reactive, emotional, or inconsistent responses from a guardian produce reactive, emotional, and inconsistent behavior in youth. Structured, calm, deliberate responses model exactly what the program is trying to build in them.

The FIRM Framework for Guardian Responses

Use this framework any time a situation requires a response from you as a guardian.

Step	What It Means	What You Do
F: FACTS FIRST	Gather the full picture before you respond	What actually happened? Do not respond to your youth's version alone, verify when possible.
I: IDENTIFY THE STANDARD	Connect the situation to the expectation	What is the program requirement? What is your home standard? Was it met or not?
R: RESPOND DELIBERATELY	Choose a structured,	What is the appropriate consequence or

	calm response	action? Apply it consistently regardless of emotion.
M: MAINTAIN AND FOLLOW THROUGH	Hold the line on your response	Do not walk back a consequence because your youth pushes back. Follow through every time.

Guardian Decision Worksheet

Use this worksheet to work through any significant situation before you respond.

What happened (facts only, not interpretation):

Which expectation or requirement was involved:

My initial emotional reaction:

The structured, appropriate response:

How I will follow through:

> KEY PRINCIPLE:

> **How you respond shapes how your youth learns to respond. The FIRM Framework gives you a structured process that stays consistent regardless of how difficult the situation is.**

SECTION 5: DAILY HOME STRUCTURE SYSTEM

Structure at home is not about being rigid. It is about being predictable. Youth in structured programs are learning to operate inside systems with consistent expectations. The home environment either reinforces that learning or undermines it. A structured home routine makes the program's job easier, and your youth's success more likely.

Daily Home Expectations. Establish These First

Before you can track anything, the expectations must be defined and communicated clearly. Use the lines below to establish the non-negotiable daily standards in your home.

Morning routine, what is required before leaving home each day:

School or program attendance, what is expected:

Curfew, time and any conditions:

Household responsibilities, what they are required to complete:

Technology and social media, any conditions or restrictions:

Check-in requirement, when and how they report to you each day:

____

____

Daily Home Structure Tracker

Use this tracker to monitor daily completion of home responsibilities and expectations.

Task / Expectation	Required Time	Completed (Y/N)	Guardian Notes

Daily Guardian Check-In

Complete this every evening as a brief review of the day.

- ☐ My youth completed their required home responsibilities today
- ☐ My youth met their curfew and all check-in requirements

- ☐ I communicated calmly and clearly with my youth today
- ☐ I held the home standard consistently. I did not make exceptions under pressure
- ☐ I am aware of where my youth was and who they were with today

> KEY PRINCIPLE:
> **Daily structure creates the stability that youth in structured programs need at home. Consistency every day is more powerful than intensity occasionally.**

SECTION 6: WEEKLY FAMILY ACCOUNTABILITY SYSTEM

Weekly accountability reviews give you and your youth a structured opportunity to assess progress, address problems, and reset expectations together. This is not a punishment session, it is a business-like review of how the week went against the standard that was set. Conduct it on the same day and at the same time every week.

Weekly Guardian Review Worksheet

Week of:

What my youth did well this week:

What needs to improve:

Any requirements that were missed and how they were addressed:

My own consistency as a guardian this week, what I held and what I let slide:

One expectation I want to reinforce specifically next week:

Weekly Accountability Tracker

Expectation / Responsibility	Status This Week	Action Taken	Follow-Up Needed

Weekly Program Communication Log

Record any communication with the program, school, or supervising authority this week.

Date	Who I Spoke With	What Was Discussed	Outcome / Next Step

> KEY PRINCIPLE:
> **Weekly accountability keeps small problems from becoming large ones. Review every week on schedule, not just when something goes wrong.**

SECTION 7: FAMILY COMMUNICATION SYSTEM

The way you communicate with your youth teaches them how to communicate with the world. Heated, inconsistent, or threatening communication at home produces youth who do not know how to regulate their communication in structured environments. Calm, clear, structured communication at home produces the opposite.

Guardian Communication Standards

- Deliver expectations clearly and once, repeating the same instruction with increasing volume teaches nothing except that volume is how authority works
- Separate the behavior from the person, correct the action, do not attack the character
- Stay calm when you deliver consequences, emotion signals that the consequence is negotiable
- Listen to your youth fully before responding, they need to feel heard even when you are holding a line
- Do not discuss program requirements in terms of your own opinion of them, your youth needs to see you supporting the structure, not critiquing it
- Follow up on what you say, if you tell your youth there will be a consequence, there must be one

How to Have a Difficult Conversation

Use this process when a conversation is likely to be emotional or contentious.

Step 1. Prepare	Know what you need to say before you start. Write it down if needed. Be clear on the expectation that was not met and the consequence that follows.
Step 2. Choose the Right Time	Do not have the conversation when either of you is activated, hungry, or distracted. Set a time, sit down, and keep the environment calm.
Step 3. State the Facts	Describe what happened factually and briefly. Do not editorialize or bring up past history unless it is directly relevant.
Step 4. State the Expectation	Be clear about what the standard is and why it matters. Connect it to the program requirement if relevant.
Step 5. State the Consequence	Be specific and calm. Consequences announced in anger are rarely applied consistently.
Step 6. Listen	Give your youth a chance to respond. You do not have to agree, but you do need to hear them.
Step 7. Close the Conversation	Confirm what was agreed, what the consequence is, and what happens next. Then end the conversation. Do not relitigate it.

Family Communication Log

Date	Topic	How It Went	What Was Agreed / Next Step

KEY PRINCIPLE:
Clear communication prevents unnecessary conflict. How you communicate with your youth is the model they use to communicate with everyone else in their structured environment.

SECTION 8: SUPPORTING WITHOUT ENABLING

This is one of the most important distinctions in this entire guide. Support and enabling look similar from the outside, both involve a guardian doing something for or because of their youth. The difference is in the outcome. Support builds capacity. Enabling removes the need to build it.

What Enabling Looks Like

- Calling your youth's program to explain why they missed a requirement instead of requiring your youth to make that call themselves
- Removing or reducing a consequence because your youth became emotional, persistent, or manipulative
- Making excuses to program staff for your youth's behavior
- Providing resources such as money, transportation, or access that enable behavior violating program conditions
- Agreeing with your youth that a requirement is unfair in a way that justifies non-compliance
- Protecting your youth from the natural consequences of their choices because the consequences are uncomfortable to witness

What Support Looks Like

- Requiring your youth to make their own calls, attend their own meetings, and address their own issues, while being present as backup when genuinely needed

- Holding consequences firmly and calmly, even when it is uncomfortable
- Reinforcing program expectations at home so your youth hears the same standard from every direction
- Providing transportation to required appointments, but not to unapproved locations
- Listening to your youth's frustrations about the program without undermining the program's authority
- Celebrating genuine progress in a way that reinforces the behavior, not just the outcome

Support vs. Enabling. Self-Check Worksheet

For each situation, record your typical response and assess whether it is support or enabling.

Situation	My Typical Response	Support or Enabling?	What I Should Do Instead

KEY PRINCIPLE:

> **Support helps growth. Enabling delays it. Every time you remove a consequence or make an excuse, you are teaching your youth that the standard does not actually apply to them.**

SECTION 9: COMMON SITUATIONS AND HOW TO HANDLE THEM

These are the situations that most commonly create conflict between families and youth in structured programs, and between families and the programs themselves. Read each one. Know the structured response before the situation arises.

Your Youth Refuses to Complete a Required Responsibility

What usually goes wrong:

Arguing repeatedly, issuing threats you will not follow through on, eventually giving up and doing it for them

The structured response:

- State the expectation once, clearly and calmly
- State the consequence once, specifically and without emotion
- Leave the space and allow them to choose
- Apply the consequence if they do not comply, without negotiation
- Do not repeat the instruction. Repeating signals that compliance is optional.

Your Youth Tells You the Program Is Being Unfair

What usually goes wrong:

Agreeing with your youth without full information, calling the program to complain on their behalf, undermining the program's authority at home

The structured response:

- Listen to your youth's concern fully before responding
- Tell your youth you will look into it, then contact the program directly to get their account
- Do not share your opinion of the program's decision until you have full information
- If there is a legitimate concern, address it through the correct formal channel
- Do not let your youth use 'unfairness' as a justification for non-compliance while the issue is being addressed

Conflict Escalates at Home

What usually goes wrong:

Escalating in return, making statements you cannot take back, allowing the conflict to become physical or threatening

The structured response:

- Stop the conversation the moment either party is no longer regulated
- State that you will continue the conversation when both of you are calm
- Remove yourself from the space if needed
- Do not threaten consequences in the heat of the moment
- Return to the conversation at a scheduled time with a clear head

Your Youth Misses a Program Requirement

What usually goes wrong:

Contacting the program to explain or excuse the miss, minimizing the significance, or blaming the program

The structured response:

- Require your youth to contact the program themselves to report the miss
- Do not offer to make the call for them unless they are genuinely incapable
- Apply any home consequence that corresponds to the miss
- Do not express sympathy for the consequence the program applies, reinforce that consequences follow choices
- Follow up to confirm the miss was reported and addressed

Your Youth Is Pressured by Peers to Violate Conditions

What usually goes wrong:

Dismissing the concern, minimizing the peer's influence, or allowing contact with individuals who are a known risk

The structured response:

- Take peer pressure seriously, it is one of the leading causes of youth violations
- Know who your youth spends time with and whether those individuals are approved contacts
- Have direct conversations about specific people and specific situations, not general lectures
- Reinforce that one decision driven by peer pressure can set back months of progress
- Support your youth in building language for declining, they need practical tools, not just principles

You Disagree with a Decision the Program Made

What usually goes wrong:

Telling your youth you disagree with the program, refusing to reinforce a program requirement you think is unreasonable

The structured response:

- Keep your disagreement away from your youth until it is resolved
- Contact the appropriate program staff directly and professionally
- Use the formal appeal or grievance process if one exists
- Continue reinforcing the requirement at home while the concern is being addressed
- Remember that undermining program authority at home is one of the most direct paths to your youth's failure

> KEY PRINCIPLE:
> **Most family-driven youth failures are predictable and preventable. The structured response to each situation can be prepared in advance. Use this section before situations arise.**

SECTION 10: RESET AND RECOVERY SYSTEM

There will be weeks where the structure breaks down, where you did not follow through, where a conflict escalated beyond where it should have, where your youth fell short of expectations and the response was inconsistent. The Reset and Recovery System gives you a structured process for getting both you and your youth back on track.

The Guardian Recovery Process

Step 1. Acknowledge What Happened	Be honest with yourself about what broke down and what your role in it was. Do not assign blame before you assess your own contribution.
Step 2. Reconnect with the Standard	Review the program requirements and your home expectations. Reestablish what the actual standard is, in your own mind first, then with your youth.
Step 3. Reset Expectations Explicitly	Have a direct conversation with your youth that resets the standard without relitigating the breakdown. State what is expected going forward, specifically.
Step 4. Re-engage with the Program	If the breakdown involved program requirements, contact the appropriate staff to understand the current status and

	what is needed to get back on track.
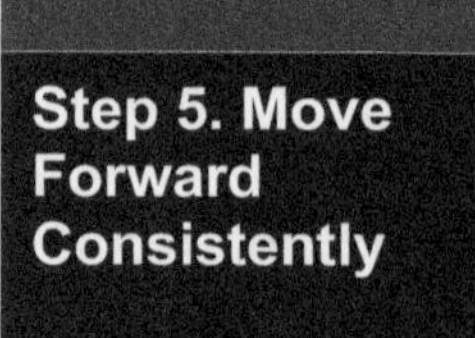 **Step 5. Move Forward Consistently**	Do not let the reset conversation become an ongoing reference point for guilt or blame. Apply the standard going forward and review it weekly.

Guardian Reset Worksheet

What broke down this week:

My role in what happened:

What the reset conversation covered:

What I will do differently going forward:

What my youth committed to going forward:

> KEY PRINCIPLE:
> **Resetting correctly prevents a single bad week from becoming a pattern. Use this process every time, for your youth and for yourself.**

SECTION 11: BUILDING CONSISTENCY OVER TIME

Consistency is not intensity. It is not being the strictest parent or the most attentive guardian every single day. It is applying the same standard, the same response, and the same follow-through across time, including the days when you are tired, stressed, or emotionally depleted. That is what makes it consistent.

What Consistency Requires

- The same expectation applies on Monday and on Friday, regardless of how the week went
- A consequence that was announced is a consequence that is applied, no exceptions based on mood or pressure
- The standard does not change because your youth had a hard day, it changes through a formal, deliberate conversation, not through erosion
- Your own self-regulation is part of the system, a guardian who cannot stay regulated cannot hold a consistent standard
- Consistency is more important than perfection, a guardian who falls short and resets correctly is more effective than one who never falls short but cannot recover

Consistency Self-Assessment. Monthly

Complete this at the end of each month alongside your Monthly Progress Review.

Area	Was I Consistent? (Y/N)	Where I Fell Short	What I Will Do Differently
Holding curfew and check-in requirements			
Following through on stated consequences			
Maintaining calm communication			
Staying aligned with program expectations			
Completing weekly reviews			
Engaging with the program when needed			

> KEY PRINCIPLE:
> **Consistency builds trust and structure. Your youth is watching what you do after you say something more than they are listening to what you say.**

SECTION 12: MONTHLY FAMILY PROGRESS SYSTEM

Monthly reviews give you a longer perspective on progress that is impossible to see day to day. Complete this review on the same day each month. If possible, complete it in coordination with any program review or reporting cycle so your assessment aligns with the program's.

Monthly Family Review Worksheet

Month reviewed:

Progress my youth made this month:

My own growth as a consistent support system this month:

Challenges we faced as a family this month:

What the program reported about my youth's progress this month:

One thing I will focus on as a guardian next month:

Monthly Goal Tracker

Goal	For Youth or Guardian	Status	Next Step

Monthly Compliance Summary

Requirement	Times Required	Times Met	Issues and How They Were Addressed

> KEY PRINCIPLE:
> **Long-term progress comes from consistent short-term effort. One strong month builds the next. Review every month without exception.**

SECTION 13: QUICK REFERENCE CHECKLISTS

Post these checklists where you will see them. Review them at the start and end of each day. Use them to hold yourself accountable, not just your youth.

Daily Guardian Checklist

- ☐ I communicated calmly and clearly with my youth today
- ☐ I held all home expectations consistently, no exceptions made under pressure
- ☐ I know where my youth was and who they were with today
- ☐ My youth completed their required home responsibilities
- ☐ I completed my Daily Guardian Check-In

Weekly Family Accountability Checklist

- ☐ I completed the Weekly Guardian Review Worksheet
- ☐ I held the weekly family accountability check-in with my youth
- ☐ I communicated with the program if anything needed to be reported
- ☐ I updated the Weekly Accountability Tracker
- ☐ I identified what I will focus on next week as a guardian

Support vs. Enabling Quick Check

- ☐ I required my youth to handle their own responsibilities. I did not do it for them
- ☐ I held consequences that were announced. I did not walk them back
- ☐ I did not make excuses to program staff for my youth's behavior
- ☐ I reinforced program expectations at home. I did not undermine them

FIRM Framework Quick Reference

- ☐ F: FACTS FIRST: Get the full picture before I respond
- ☐ I: IDENTIFY THE STANDARD: Connect the situation to the expectation
- ☐ R: RESPOND DELIBERATELY: Choose a structured, calm response
- ☐ M: MAINTAIN AND FOLLOW THROUGH: Hold the line every time

> KEY PRINCIPLE:
> **These checklists hold you accountable the same way the workbooks hold your youth accountable. Use them every day.**

A FINAL WORD

Your youth has a program working with them. They have counselors and staff and case managers. What they do not have anywhere else is a parent or guardian who shows up consistently, holds the standard firmly, and loves them enough to let consequences do their work.

That is your role. No program can replicate it. No staff member can replace it.

Use this guide every day. Your consistency is the foundation your youth builds everything else on.

North Star Practical Guides

www.ingramcontent.com/pod-product-compliance
Lightning Source LLC
LaVergne TN
LVHW010945110826
845149LV00013B/2764

* 9 7 9 8 9 9 6 0 7 1 4 4 9 *